Dear
Stefan,
Hope this book
feeds your artistic
+ creative spirit. Enjoy!
Happy Birthday!
In love & friendship
Linda

Bonsai

Christine Stewart

Bonsai
a step-by-step guide

LONGMEADOW
PRESS

Half title page — *Flowering japonica (ornamental quince) in the cascade style.*
Title page — *A 250-year-old Chinese juniper, a rare specimen bonsai.*
This page — *Informal upright mountain maple in spectacular autumn foliage.*

Published by Longmeadow Press, 201 High Ridge Road, Stamford, CT 06904. All rights reserved. No part of this book may be reproduced or utilized in any form or by any means, electronic or mechanical, including photocopying, recording or by any information storage and retrieval system, without permission in writing from the Publisher.

ISBN: 0-681-45416-4
Printed in The Slovak Republic
First Longmeadow Press Edition 1993
0 9 8 7 6 5 4 3 2 1

Contents

The Art of Bonsai

Bonsai, despite their exotic connotations, are simply miniature trees raised in small pots. Not to be confused with genetically dwarfed varieties of tree which remain the same size without any help from the grower, bonsai are tiny replicas of their full-grown brethren in forest and garden, formed over the years by man's patience and skill. Contrary to general belief, no esoteric techniques are employed in bonsai culture. Despite their far-flung ancestry — bonsai is the Japanese word for a plant in a pot — and many misconceptions, the little trees are created not by savagery or starvation but by everyday gardening methods such as pruning and potting.

Yet a faithful small-scale reproduction of any tree will not necessarily capture the spirit of bonsai, which is to encapsulate, in a container, a memorable aspect of nature. Bonsai are, in fact, stylized forms of trees in the wild, the relationship of the miniature to its shallow container playing an integral part in creating the overall impression of unity. And, to be worthy of the name, good bonsai should combine the effects of trunk, branches, leaves, flowers and fruit in a totally harmonious whole. A dwarfed juniper with twisted trunk and shapely branch structure, a tiny azalea in full bloom, a maple bonsai covered in the multi-coloured leaves of autumn, all convey the beauty of wild trees in their natural environment in a condensed and spectacular form.

Age in bonsai is no prerequisite of quality. Neither is cost nor the extent of miniaturization. Measured from the base of the trunk to the tip, bonsai range from the tiny trees known as *mame* bonsai — up to 15 centimetres (6 inches) high — to the really tall ones which can grow to a height of over 90 centimetres (3 feet). The latter will take many years to achieve true beauty but a mame bonsai may be delightful within three years, and a fast-growing medium-sized tree of about 50 centimetres (20 inches) should make a very acceptable bonsai after eight to ten years' training.

Indeed, one of the joys of bonsai is that they can be grown from seed or taken from the wild

Informal upright pyracantha in colourful autumn berry. A popular bonsai tree, the 'firethorn', as it is commonly known, differs from its relative, the cotoneaster in that it has thorny branches. Photographed in May, this particular tree is unusual as it was bearing fruit formed the previous September.

by relatively inexperienced beginners. Certainly, reserves of patience will be called upon while the seedlings mature, but the enthusiast can start work immediately on a wild tree, achieving noticeable results in a comparatively short period.

Nor should a bonsai which is undistinguished as an individual tree be dismissed out of hand. A lone pine of indifferent shape, for instance, can take on new meaning if grouped with others on a shallow tray or arranged to form part of a scene in a miniature garden. These gardens, unlike the deep tub and sink versions, offer interest in their skilful use of perspective combined with an overall simplicity of design. By carefully positioning a conifer, say, or a windswept style of tree in relation to attractive rocks, sand and moss, a whole scene can be recaptured in a limited space. Similarly, a number of saplings planted in forest-like profusion on a large oval tray can be very effective, masking the immaturity that would be obvious in individual bonsai and recreating a much-loved landscape.

Newcomers to bonsai, who fear their lack of artistic talent, should not be deterred by the emphasis placed on aesthetic appreciation; a well-developed sense of design should be considered a bonus but is not essential. Flower-arrangers, for instance, may more easily comprehend the basic relationships of shapes, proportions and colours of bonsai, but everyone can learn from looking at established trees in city parks and squares as well as in the open countryside. It is no exaggeration to say that working with bonsai offers something to everyone, from those who enjoy any aspect of gardening to those with the highest artistic aspirations.

There are problems, of course, but these are usually due to lack of experience. Because bonsai are small they are commonly mistaken for indoor plants. In fact, they should simply remain in whatever conditions are natural to growth. Tropical bonsai, therefore, which would obviously flourish in tropical climates, might well, like houseplants, grow well indoors. The majority of bonsai, however, are accustomed to growing outside in temperate weather and are quite happy exposed to the elements in the garden or on the patio. Evergreen bonsai go through a semi-dormant period and deciduous species drop their leaves in the autumn—facts frequently not appreciated by tender-hearted owners who rush the trees inside at the first sign of a cold snap, often to a centrally-heated death.

A pyracantha in full bloom in the early summer. This shrub is noted for its spectacular blossom, similar to that of the hawthorn. The varying display throughout the seasons makes the pyracantha an excellent subject for bonsai, especially as it is quick-growing, hardy and happy in most fertile soils.

Similarly, over-watering or excessive feeding can be equally destructive and errors of pruning may take years to correct.

Such initial problems are more than offset by the lasting pleasure to be derived from bonsai. Enthusiasm for the dwarfed trees is frequently accompanied by a widening knowledge of trees in general, so that even those in urban environments take on greater significance. An increased awareness of other aspects of the countryside often results too. Above all, cultivating miniature trees is a calming activity which, apart from the intrinsic satisfaction of growing bonsai at home, provides an added therapeutic and relaxing bonus. The shape of the trees, the texture of the bark, the colour and scents of the flowers and foliage, all speak for themselves in what can only be referred to as a living, constantly changing work of art.

Are there no snags, then? Very few, apart from those encountered in the ordinary horticultural practices of potting and pruning, feeding and watering and so on. But be warned, growing bonsai is not for those unprepared to devote just a few minutes a day to their hobby. High standards of health and care are needed, along with an enquiring mind in working out what is best for certain trees. In short, be prepared to combine strong self-discipline with a practical streak and an unfettered imagination.

An ability to compromise is perhaps even more essential. A bonsai can sometimes offer scope far beyond that suggested by initial impressions, so be prepared to 'file away' a new tree for a few months until new growth may suggest other possibilities. Learn as much as possible from books and experts, but always keep an open mind. The very best bonsai are beautiful in their own right, not necessarily because they observe set forms. Respect the disciplines of the Japanese masters, but do not be limited by hard and fast rules supposedly laid down by them. Bear these precepts in mind at all times to gain great satisfaction and enrichment from a comparatively simple and not necessarily expensive hobby.

Project 1
Bonsai from a Nursery Beech

As recommended earlier, an excellent way to begin growing bonsai is to buy one or two young trees with potential for training as miniatures from a good general nursery (see Chapter 3). Many species fall into this category, including maple, cotoneaster and flowering shrubs such as azalea and laburnum. A wise popular choice would be one of the varieties of beech with its graceful structure, grey bark and bronze winter foliage. Being much in demand for hedging, beech is widely stocked by most garden centres.

One disadvantage of such commonly available trees, however, is that the sheer weight of numbers of any one variety in a single nursery can prove confusing to the beginner who may thus fail to recognize a good potential bonsai. To avoid this, whenever possible take along an interested friend who does not have preconceived ideas about what makes a bonsai and will see the trees with a fresh eye. Do not automatically reject those trees which, at first glance, seem hopelessly inadeqate for what you have in mind. For instance, a tree which has fallen over and remained on its side for a long time, may have developed a particularly one-sided branch system which could be trained as a cascade or waterfall bonsai. Above all keep an open mind,

concentrating on what the trees have to offer rather than what you would like to create, and you may receive a pleasant surprise.

At the beginning, however, you may opt for an informal upright style, perhaps the simplest shape for those first attempting bonsai culture. Although immature, the chosen tree should possess certain characteristics which indicate that it is good bonsai material. Look first at the trunk: a straight trunk, tapering gradually to the crown from a good, firm base is essential for this style. Avoid trunks with an ugly, waisted effect — a common fault in container-grown trees — or those with undesirable bends too near the base.

It is often difficult to estimate the length of trunk on trees such as cotoneasters which are nearly always well buried in the pot with lots of foliage spreading deceptively above. If in doubt, run a hand gently down the trunk to find out exactly where it meets the soil. If there is a reasonably long trunk, providing that other features are right, the tree may make a good bonsai cotoneaster.

Use a similar technique to assess the state of the roots. Sometimes plants are left too long in their original plastic or peat pots before they are transplanted into the larger containers in which

Left: The beech, purchased in early autumn, still in its plastic nursery container. About 30 cm (12 in) high, the little tree has a good long trunk which should thicken out well over the years. It also has a well-spaced branch structure which, although a little top heavy and one-sided at the moment, has potential for training.

Overleaf: The outstanding feature of this beech bonsai is its striking root formation. So strong and shapely are the roots that they appear as an extension of the trunk. The style of the top balances the tree's unusual base.

Step 1

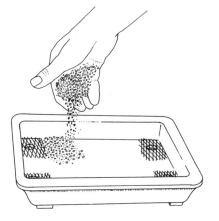

To prepare the new container, first cover the drainage holes with fine-mesh material such as the plastic garden netting which is widely available. Add a layer of drainage matter (as shown) such as fish tank gravel, obtainable from your local pet store. Use a soil mix recommended by the nurseryman, adding leaf-mould and sand as necessary according to the type of tree. Sterilize the soil and sieve it to a running consistency, then add it to the container.

Step 2

Take the tree and its rootball cleanly from the original container, either by cutting away the plastic or tapping lightly from beneath. Holding the tree firmly at the base of its trunk, shake off any excess soil and, using a small rake, carefully tease out any roots which have wound round themselves. If the root system is well developed, cut it back lightly all round so that a compact rootball with a heavy fringe of roots remains.

Step 3

Place the tree towards the rear of the prepared container, positioning it slightly to left or right of the centre line. If the tree favours the right, with its most prominent branches on that side, then put it on the left of the container and vice versa. Anchor it firmly in place with one hand, heaping up soil around the roots with the other until the compost is within 2 cm (about 1 in) of the rim of the pot.

Step 4

After six months or so in its bonsai container the tree has put on new growth, benefiting from the previous light pruning to develop a much more bushy outline. Marks indicate where the next pruning should be done to encourage growth on the side branches and keep down vigorous top growth which is undesirable.

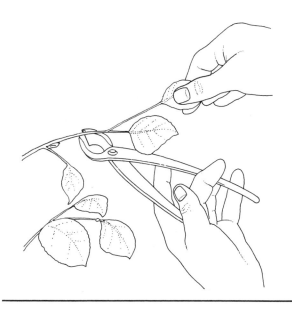

Step 5

To branch prune, take the unwanted part of the branch in one hand, holding it apart from the rest of the foliage so that you can see clearly what you are doing. With the pruners, snip off the over-length twig, just above an up- or downward-facing bud, depending on the desired direction of growth.

Step 6

The top growth has been cut back severely to enable the side branches to become stronger. Continue this regular light pruning until the tree has developed enough to be potted down into a smaller container, when the rootball will again be trimmed back. At this stage, in certain cases, the tree will become top-heavy in relation to its rootball, and should be kept in place by fine wires running over its base and through the drainage holes to be secured underneath the container, thus preventing it from snapping in strong winds.

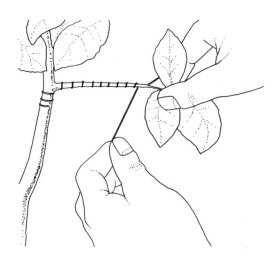

Step 7

When the young tree can be seen to be growing well and is on the way to a good overall shape, any wayward branches can be eased into position by gentle wiring. Here, a side branch is being brought down to give an impression of age. Anchor the wire round the trunk for stability, then wind the wire evenly round the branch at a regular distance, exerting just enough pressure to hold the branch in place. Setting time varies according to the season, species and size of branch being trained, but do remove the wire as soon as it looks too tight and rewire if necessary.

they will be sold. This means that the roots are unable to grow down and instead turn upwards, winding round and round the rootball so that eventually they become pot-bound. In a young tree, such circular roots can be unravelled with care, but they are virtually immoveable in a mature specimen.

Ideally, bonsai roots should radiate from the trunk base in a clear, untangled manner. As it is usually difficult to see the roots of very young trees, when a possible purchase has been singled out, poke gently down into the soil with an index finger; if you can feel the rim of the smaller pot still in there, do not buy that tree, however appealing. The nursery staff will not object to this amateur detective work so long as it is done in moderation and with care. They heap soil over the base of trees to retain moisture, particularly in large establishments where automatic watering is employed, so are not trying to hide the roots in any way.

Select a well-branched tree, not a single shoot. If you are going to create an informal upright style with alternating branches on either side of the trunk, reject trees with either branches growing opposite each other at the same level, with branches low down on the trunk, or with branches forming a cartwheel structure round the trunk. A common fault in nursery stock is a trunk with very few branches near the base. Although such trees might be perfectly acceptable in a group planting where a dozen or so tall trees would look very effective, it would be most frustrating for a novice to attempt to train one as an individual tree. In the same way, a branch too low down on the trunk will detract from its acceptability as a good bonsai.

Equally, a heavy top branch at this early stage will only cause long-term problems. It is relatively simple to encourage tops of trees to grow — a young tree will always look very upright as spreading only comes with maturity — but more difficult to make low branches thicken, so a tree which starts off top-heavy may only grow more so.

Having selected and purchased the tree, in this case a beech, carefully transport it home. However much you may itch to start work on it immediately, try to contain your impatience for a day or so and learn simply to live with the tree, studying its shape from all angles and deciding how best to tackle it. When you feel confident about the basic shape, give it a preliminary prune, cutting back over-long shoots to achieve a tidier overall outline. If you are trying to make

the branches grow down to give an impression of age, prune to an underneath bud (see figures 22 and 23).

After a week or so, when the tree has recovered from any shocks caused by the change of locale and the initial pruning, it can be transferred from its plastic pot to a more permanent home. Choose a proper bonsai pot so as to begin creating a flat rootball, but at this early stage use a fairly deep one which can accommodate the present rootball without too much radical pruning. Prepare the container as shown in Step 1 and described in detail in figure 20.

The simplest way to take the young tree from a plastic grow-pot, without disturbing the roots is simply to cut away the pot all around. If the tree is in an earthenware planter, however, allow the soil mix to become fairly dry then turn the pot carefully upside down and tap sharply on the base a couple of times to release both soil and rootball. *Never* attempt to lift any plant by its stem or trunk as it may simply break, or to loosen soil from the top as this may damage roots growing upwards.

With the rootball duly prepared (Step 2), place the tree in its container as shown in Step 3. Water thoroughly by standing the pot up to its rim in water until the soil surface glistens. Put the tree outside in a sheltered position, preferably in the shade of a larger tree but receiving some sunlight. As the roots become established over a three to four week period, the tree can gradually be brought into full sunlight. It should never again be necessary to water the tree by near total immersion, unless the soil has dried out completely due to unforeseen circumstances. Simply spray the leaves regularly to prevent transpiration and water only often enough to keep the rootball moist, as sodden roots tend to rot.

After a season's growth, prune lightly as shown in Steps 4 and 5. At this stage the container will still look too big for the tree, but health is more important than beauty in this initial period while the rootball becomes truly established. Years may pass before a satisfactory balance is achieved between tree and pot, by which time the nursery fledgling should be worthy of the name of bonsai. During this time, by regular pruning of rootball and branches (Step 6), repotting and training by wiring (Step 7 and figure 29), you will have learned far more by practical application than can be gleaned from any book. Now you will be creating more bonsai, in varying styles from different species

The young beech seen at the beginning of this project, branch-pruned and potted into a proper bonsai container, shows what can be achieved with basic knowledge and skill in 6—8 months.

and by extensions to the basic methods with which you are already familiar.

British and American bonsai societies are now actively encouraging the idea of growing native trees from nurseries as bonsai. However, it must be remembered that simply putting a tree in a pot and pruning it back here and there will not create a bonsai; only many years of careful training will result in the mature specimens which are regarded as true bonsai by the Japanese.

Project 2
Wild Pine Bonsai

Stunted, sinuous trees in the wild have already been described as Nature's own bonsai, their dwarf size and unusual shape being directly attributable to an alien environment caused, in the main, by poor soil and inclement weather. Such trees may also have been subjected to regular pruning by various animals in their search for food. However formed, there is little doubt that such shapely miniatures were the very first bonsai, being avidly dug up and cultivated first by the Chinese and later by wealthy Japanese who organized frequently perilous bonsai-collecting expeditions.

Although there is no need to go to such lengths today, selecting a wild tree to train as a bonsai can still be a fairly hazardous process, particularly in digging up the tree and ensuring that it survives, though the rewards can be equally great. Keep your eyes open for suitable specimens when walking through woods. You may not need to wander too far off the beaten track as stunted trees are often found close to the path, thoughtlessly trodden on by other walkers some years earlier and surviving in a misshapen form. Moorlands may also yield potential bonsai which have become stunted by growing in an exposed position. Look for young trees which will not object to being dug up and can only benefit from training. Do not be tempted by very contorted trees or those with lots of deadwood, as they are usually very old and will not take kindly to attempts to transplant them.

Many wild trees such as beech, larch, oak and pine can be trained as bonsai, provided that some precautions are taken when removing the tree from its natural habitat. Apart from the practicalities of obtaining permission to remove plants from private land, you cannot simply find a suitable tree one day and remove it the next, unless it is the right time of year.

The best time to take trees from the wild is just before their leaves are due to open, usually in spring, though the exact month or even week may vary according to geographical location. Never move deciduous trees when their leaves are unfolding as this nearly always kills them. If you have not been able to move the tree at the swelling bud stage, if possible leave it until the

Twisted by wind and weather so that its trunk and branches form a most curious yet harmonious whole, this Jeffrey pine at Sentinel Dome, Yosemite National Park, California, USA, is a stunning example of how the forces of Nature form bonsai in the wild.

21

same time the following year. It may well be, however, that the tree must be moved at a later time as the land is being cleared for building or agricultural purposes. In this case, dig up the tree, then take a pair of scissors and cut away two-thirds of every leaf. This lowers the rate of transpiration and puts less stress on the root system to draw up water. Do not take away all the leaf as cutting off at a node forces new growth which puts more strain on the roots.

The Scots pine, taken from its natural home and its rootball trimmed, has been potted at the start of its bonsai training. The top of the trunk and the branches have been wired gently but it has not yet been pruned.

Conifers can also be moved with some success in late summer when the soil is still warm and the trees have time to grow a new root system before the winter frosts. It is not advisable to lift deciduous trees at this time, however, even though cutting back the leaves will increase their chance of survival.

When going on a tree hunting foray, take care not to disturb the surrounding area by driving vehicles over cultivated ground or damaging other seedlings with heavy tools and equipment. Depending on the size of the tree, you need a spade and fork or trowel, long-handled secateurs to cut an obstinate tap root and a pair of small secateurs to trim away other extra-long, thick roots. You will also need some wet sphag-

Step 1

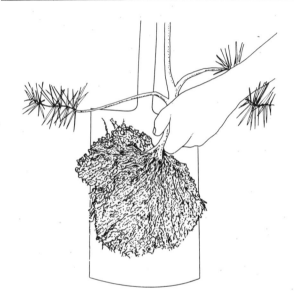

When taking trees from the wild, dig deep to make sure of obtaining a good rootball. Try to retain as much soil as possible, taken from deep in the earth where it is sterile and does not contain humus. Here the tap root has been cut back leaving the tree with a still large but manageable rootball.

Step 2

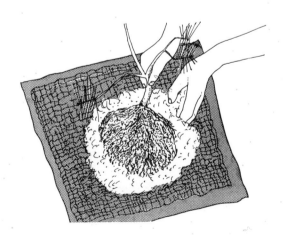

Prepare the pine for its journey home by placing it on a large sheet of polythene covered with coarse netting to secure the roots. Cut off any really long roots and pack damp sphagnum moss around the rootball to keep it moist over a long period.

Step 3

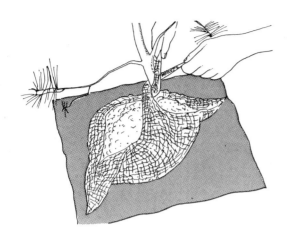

Tie up the rootball firmly but not too tightly and take the tree home as quickly as possible. On a long car journey, spray the leaves regularly to keep the tree cool. If it is very sunny, drop a polythene bag or sheet over the tree and spray beneath it from time to time so that the tree is enclosed in suitably humid conditions.

Step 4

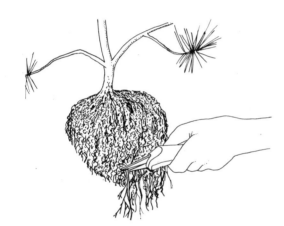

Before potting the tree, root prune gently to avoid further disturbing the roots, simply trimming any torn ones back to a clean edge. Even when trimmed, the rootball will be much larger than that of a young nursery tree and must be accommodated in a large container.

Step 5

Note how the tree is situated close to the rear of this deep plant pot. So long as all the roots fit easily into the pot, however, the position of the tree is not too important at this stage. Holding the tree firmly in one hand, make sure that the soil is well distributed around the roots, pressing it down with a chopstick.

Step 6

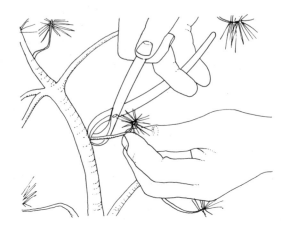

Cut off unwanted branches close to the trunk. Use of the correct Japanese branch pruning tool will leave a concave cut in the trunk. This helps the bark to grow over smoothly so that an unobtrusive flat scar remains instead of an ugly protruberance.

Step 7

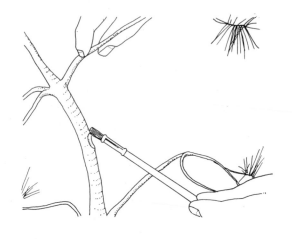

Help the scar to heal quickly and avoid infection, particularly if the cut is a large one, by painting the 'wound' with a special compound. The branded variety used on outdoor fruit trees after pruning is perfectly acceptable. Pines, however, may bleed when cut so soon after being uprooted and, in this case, the 'wound' is best cauterized.

Step 8

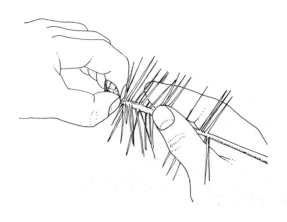

An effective method of pruning conifers when once the basic shape has been established is by pinching out the growing buds. Taking care to select the right branches, simply nip out the new buds between thumb and forefinger. This leaves an undamaged tip and encourages side growth. Do not cut across the tip, as this leaves an ugly brown stump which takes time to recover and restricts more useful growth.

num moss, a large piece of polythene, and string to tie up the tree securely for safe and easy transportation.

On site, clear away surface rubbish from around the tree then, looking down on it, mark out a circle about the size of the tree's crown. It is remarkable how deep even young roots may go, so dig well down around the circle to free the rootball (Step 1). Take care to inflict as little harm as possible to the roots and branches, securely parcelling up the tree for its journey home and creating a moist environment for it, as described in Steps 2 and 3.

A wild tree should be potted as soon as is feasible to minimize the shock of its being taken from the ground and moved. First, cut back any remaining taproot and other extraneous shoots, leaving a border of smaller roots around the rootball. The main object now is to keep the tree healthy while it develops a new root system, so do not attempt to restrict the rootball within a conventional shallow bonsai container but prepare a suitably large plant pot or deep seed box, retaining as much of the original soil around the roots as possible. The remaining soil should contain a mixture of ingredients — peat, loam, leaf-mould, etc. — particularly suited to the type of tree. For instance, a preponderance of sand in the soil mixture will be appreciated by pines.

Pines are popular bonsai trees the world over. The Japanese white pine *(Pinus parviflora)* is much used in that country as it adapts so easily to the classic pine style and many others. In Britain, the Scots pine *(Pinus sylvestris),* as used in this project, is a common bonsai tree, but it needs handling with special care when taking from the wild as roots may 'bleed' when severed and should ideally be cauterized if the pine is to survive with any degree of success.

When the wild tree is securely potted in its temporary container, to help the roots re-establish themselves in their new home in the shortest possible time, take away part of their workload by removing any branches which are superfluous to the basic shape, as in Step 6. If you do not have a proper branch pruner which makes a concave cut, simply take the branch off flush

The incredibly curved trunk of this blossoming hawthorn has the extravagance of the wandering literati-style bonsai. The excessive trunk was formed in the wild, where it was found growing beside a windswept path, then potted and trained as a bonsai.

After a year, the pine from the wild is beginning to look much more like a bonsai. It has been pruned regularly to achieve a more compact shape, though the branches remain wired to bring them down more in keeping with an older tree. It has been repotted and positioned against a large rock which is used as a feature to create the impression of the pine growing in a natural environment.

with the trunk, then use a sharp knife to carve out a circular scar. This will enable the bark to grow over as neatly as if a concave cut had been made originally.

The tree can now be placed outside and moved gradually into full sunlight. Conifers which have not adapted to their new home soon show symptoms of distress such as dehydrated needles. Make sure that such trees are in well-drained soil and increase the humidity by placing them in a cold frame or blowing up a polythene bag and putting it over them. Do not be misled into thinking that the trees need feeding as fertilizer will burn damaged roots which tend to rot in over-rich soil.

Depending on the individual tree, the time of year and the weather, it should start to put on new growth within a matter of months. Do not attempt to repot it at this stage as it can take up to a year for the new rootball to become established. A little light training can commence, however, after a few months, so long as the tree is obviously healthy. Wire any wayward branches lightly and evenly in place as described in Chapter 6 (figure 29). Think of the ideal shape in relation to the correct bonsai container and, if it helps, tilt the pot so that the branch is at the right angle before wiring.

Later, when potting down to contain the new rootball within the confines of a smaller pot, you may discover that the rootball and the wired branches are at very different angles, so that potting the tree in the usual upright position would only result in the branches being entirely misplaced. To avoid this discrepancy, trim the rootball and pot the tree at an angle so that its branches do not look too out of place. Then, when potting on to the final bonsai container in a year or so, the rootball can be positioned correctly and the branches should be well on their way to achieving the desired shape. Thereafter, all that is needed is the customary root and crown pruning, plus general care and repotting every few years, to keep the wild tree an acceptable, if not spectacular, mature bonsai.

Project 3
Rock-clinging Maple Bonsai

Rock-clinging bonsai are ideal for beginners who are already training one or two informal upright trees and wish to create new styles at the same time as learning different techniques. Relatively simple to produce, bonsai with roots clutching rocks look most impressive, recalling scenes of trees perched perilously on a mountain-side or above a cascading waterfall.

As the rock is the corner-stone of this miniature scene, it is well worth taking the time and trouble to build up a reserve of suitable pieces of stone. Large, jagged upright rocks are popular, but size is really immaterial as certain trees benefit from being dwarfed by their setting whereas others play a dominant role. Shape too depends on the impression that is being created: a long, relatively flat rock would be successful as a plateau or an island, and a rounder, taller one would perhaps best represent a hillside.

In general, rocks for use with bonsai should have interesting shape and texture and possibly colour. Look for them in old quarries and on any stoney ground, discarding very smooth stones, however attractive they may be, as the bonsai roots must have a rough surface to cling to. (Do not use rocks from the seashore unless they have been left to weather in a garden for at least two years so that all the salts have been leached out of them.) Porous rock is well worth searching for as it reduces the need for daily watering. And, whatever its other attributes, it is most important that the rock contains at least one cavity large enough to hold the tree.

Do not despair, however, if you find a rock of the ideal shape and size but lacking any indentations in which the roots can anchor themselves. Simply take a chisel and tap lightly with a hammer to chip away small pieces of the rock, thus making the necessary holes and 'ravines'. If confined to a city with no chance of collecting natural rocks, experiment with old bricks, cracking them in large pieces and again scoring the surface with a chisel. And, if all else fails, or you are seeking a definite shape for a particular effect, why not make it yourself from cement or concrete? In this way you can control size, shape and texture, and even drill holes exactly where the roots are to lie.

Many trees are suited to the rock-clinging style, so long as they can be persuaded to grow good long roots. Encourage them by planting the baby bonsai at the top of a deep container, as narrow as possible, so that the roots have plenty of room to go straight down and not wind themselves around as they would in a shallow container. Those intending to produce several bonsai in this style might find it useful to construct a deep box with slatted sides which can be built up layer by layer as the roots extend. Beginners might prefer to utilize more mundane objects such as an old plastic bucket, so long as adequate drainage is provided.

When the roots have grown long enough to extend just below the chosen rock, it is time to decide how the rock should best be viewed to create the desired effect. Try to see how the tree will look in different positions on the rock. Do not automatically place it at the pinnacle or on an obvious plateau in the middle. A small tree, for instance, may look most natural if planted in a crevice on the rock side. When the best site has been found, hold the tree in place, spreading out the roots and cutting away any short ones which do not reach the rock base. You will need both hands to secure the roots in position, so tie the tree temporarily in place if it is at all unstable.

It is not advisable simply to spread out the roots and cover them with the clay and peat mixture (Steps 5 and 8) without first fixing them to the rock with wires. For this you will need several lengths of fine wire, about 15 cm (6 in) long, and a lead 'weight' to sink the wires in the rock cavities. Make your own sinker (Step 3) and press home the wires with a punch or nail (Step 4). Should the rock have a hard, smooth surface which prevents you from sinking the wires in this way, simply glue them in place with an epoxy resin adhesive.

With the roots anchored to the rock and placed in a relatively deep temporary container (Steps 8 and 9), it is a good idea to tie up the sphagnum moss with twine as this prevents the moss from being washed away in heavy storms,

Left: The roots of the trident maple knit together, to make this an ideal tree for training in a rock-clinging style. This maple differs from the more common Japanese maple in that its leaves are divided into three. Easily cultivated, it lives to a ripe old age, as demonstrated by these thick, gnarled, trunk-like roots. (The marks made by wires that were left too long are still noticeable on the base of the trunk.)

Overleaf: This fine Japanese maple in its autumn colours, was originally considered to be a rather flawed bonsai because of its forked trunk, despite its shapely crown. Growing it over a rock has made a feature of the split trunk which is still unusual, but looks quite natural.

Step 1

To train the young tree's roots to grow very long so that they can eventually cling to the rock, plant the baby maple at the top of a deep receptacle full of compost. A large plant pot or an old bucket make perfect containers so long as they have adequate drainage holes. Ensure, too, that there is a good layer of drainage material in soil of this depth.

Step 2

After a year or so when the roots have grown long enough, carefully take out the tree and remove all the soil from the roots. Find the best place for the tree by holding it in different positions on the rock. With the bonsai temporarily in position, spread out the roots over the rock and note where they can best be attached to the surface.

Step 3

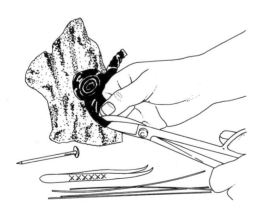

Use very fine wires to fasten the roots to the rough-textured rock. Secure the wires with lead 'sinkers', made by cutting pieces of lead foil — the weight of foil used on the tops of spirits bottles is best — in thin strips about 1 cm ($\frac{1}{2}$ in) long.

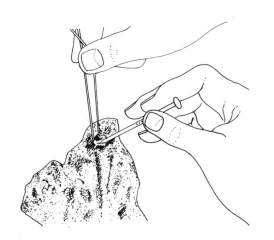

Step 4

Fold several 15 cm (6in) lengths of the wire in half and twist the foil strips round the middle, bending them to the shape of the rock cavities. Position the wires on the rock so that they can be tied round the roots and use a long nail to push the foil sinkers firmly into the surface holes.

Step 5

After mixing together equal parts of clay and peat, use a finger or small trowel to push the mixture into the places in the rock where the roots will lie. This 'soil' mix, which should be wet but not runny, will give the roots something to cling to and feed on.

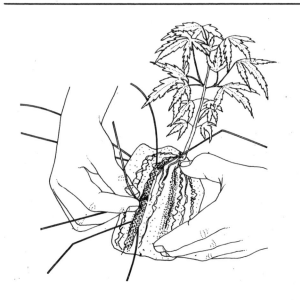

Step 6

Position the tree on the rock and spread out the roots so that they hang over the crevices of clay. As it takes time to arrange the roots correctly, prevent them from drying out by spraying occasionally with cool water. Anchor the roots firmly by tying the wire round them as securely as possible, but not so tight as to cause bruising. Knot the wire and trim off any excess.

Step 7

With the tree and roots in position, take the remaining clay/peat mix and use it to cover all the roots from top to bottom, preferably to a depth of about 1 cm (½ in). Do not skimp this operation, even though it is messy, as the roots must have some form of sustenance and cover.

Step 8

Prepare a container just slightly wider than the base of the rock and about a third as deep as the rock. Start with the usual layers of drainage material and basic soil mix. Taking care to lift the whole rock, rather than just the slender tree, put it in the container. Heap up the soil around the bottom of the roots and about a third of the way up the rock to protect it to that point.

Step 9

Pack damp sphagnum moss around the top of the rock where the roots are still exposed. This moss, which should always be kept moist with regular spraying, prevents the clay from drying out or being blown away.

It is possible to cultivate another version of the rock-clutching style by growing the trees actually in the rock cavities so that no other container is needed. This wandering holm oak (left), with the smaller branch coming off the trunk to the left, admirably suits this method, and the rough, shapely rock is a perfect vessel. The same technique has been used in the unusual decorative shell-shaped rock (below left) in which the roots of the jasmine are planted. To create the effect of a little garden, soil and moss are heaped up over the top and down the sides of the rock which contains water in the hollow so that the trees appear to be perched above a small pool.

or being blown away in hot weather if it has been allowed to dry out. Then put the container outside in a sheltered position, gradually bringing it into full sunlight as usual, but always protecting it from the wind. Apart from checking from time to time to see that the moss is damp, and occasionally spraying the leaves, do not disturb the tree for about a year. Once the roots have grasped the rock they must not be separated or they will die, so try to resist any temptation to see whether or not they have taken.

After a year, the roots should have become established. The moss can then be removed and any remaining clay washed off, revealing the strong, sinuous roots attached to the rock. (If, on taking away the first lump of moss, it is obvious that the roots have not taken, wait a further six months or so before looking again.) The rock-clinging bonsai is now ready to be potted in a permanent shallow container. Prepare the container in the usual way and position the rock securely in it, covering the ends of the long roots with compost so that they have a firm base.

As the tree ages, the roots will continue to thicken until they become as strong a feature as those of the maple illustrated at the beginning of this project. Continue to care for the tree by the usual methods, employing pruning and training techniques as necessary and repotting whenever appropriate.

Project 4
Raft Bonsai

Raft bonsai, as the name implies, is a style where several apparent trees are anchored in a sea of earth and moss by a thick, platform-like root. If this single root is not prominent, the raft may sometimes appear to be a group planting in its own right, with sinuous trunks and full crowns creating the impression of at least a copse, if not a whole forest (see Project 5). Similarly, the less well-informed sometimes confuse raft bonsai with the multi-trunk styles popular in Japan, where twin, triple and even more trunks spring from a single base.

All three styles are, in fact, quite discernibly different: *individual* trees are planted to give a group effect; in, say, a twin-trunked bonsai, the two crowns are but part of one sub-divided trunk; whereas the essential feature of a raft is the single, long root. Perhaps the style closest to this is the root-connected bonsai, again more common in Japan than in the West. Such trees occur in the wild, blown over or uprooted in a storm but remaining alive although lying on their side.

Such trees respond to the dim light which is filtered through other trees, by throwing out those branches nearest the light to form individual trunks. The crushed branches on the other side die back and the old trunk itself puts down roots to support the new branch-trunks.

Mature trees of this formation can quite often be found in exposed woodlands, but it is unusual to find young root-connected trees capable of being trained as bonsai. The raft has therefore been developed as the man-made version of this natural phenomenon. In simple terms, the tree is potted horizontally so that the old trunk sends down roots and its branches grow up as new trunks. Eventually, as the old trunk thickens and sends down roots and the new branch-trunks put on more growth, a very impressive type of island bonsai is formed.

Be warned; a raft will take years to create, and once again it is best to have other trees to cultivate while the raft is becoming established and putting on growth. Also, if you are in a hurry, do not choose a wild tree. Although most wild species are capable of being trained as rafts, they do have a major disadvantage in that

Although it looks at first as if several junipers are growing together here, this is in fact a powerful raft bonsai springing from a single root. The tree is very old and has been subjected to some rather harsh training, or perhaps merely neglect. It is now being worked on to achieve its full potential.

they will possess a well-developed rootball. This large, usually round rootball will, of course, be superfluous when the tree is turned on its side to make the raft. Indeed, such a rootball frequently makes it impossible to begin a raft style straight away. Ideally, a wild tree should simply have its rootball trimmed to avoid undue shock after being moved, then be trained for at least a year in a shallow bonsai container so that it learns to survive with a smaller root which will be less bulky when training commences.

For this reason, it is better to pick a young nursery tree which has a less developed rootball and its branches will also be more pliable. Choose an upright species as spreading shrubs, such as certain varieties of cotoneasters with their many small branches and very small leaves, will not adapt to the raft style. And look for a tree with a relatively straight trunk as this will take root more easily when it is turned sideways than a sinuous trunk which refuses to be covered by the potting soil.

For once, you are not looking for a tree with a good potential shape, nor does it need to show signs of an abundant crown. Rather, so long as the tree is obviously growing well, it is preferable if the majority of its branches grow out straight from the trunk, favouring one side. It is these branches which will eventually form the new trunks.

Before lightly wiring the branches so that they are all pointing out from the trunk in one direction (Step 2), take off any which will detract from the raft's progress, such as any well-developed branches on the 'wrong' side and any skimpy ones on the preferred side which might not keep pace with the general growth. If any of the remaining branches are out of step with their fellows, say too long or with curved tips, prune them back so that they are all approximately the same length.

When first potting the raft, the aim is to encourage it to put down roots suitable for bonsai cultivation in the shortest time possible. You should therefore use a fairly shallow container, even if it looks quite bizarre at this early stage with about half the old rootball appearing above the soil at one end (Step 3). Some practitioners recommend cutting off the mass of the rootball to begin with so it does not show, simply burying the rest; but there is a chance that the raft might well die if deprived of the majority of its original roots so early.

Do not expect the new root to become established without any outside help. All trunks will

Step 1

The young larch, still in its plastic pot as purchased from the nursery, is a healthy but unbalanced tree. Note how the majority of its branches grow to the right, with only the odd thin one on the left of the trunk. Though possessing almost no potential for any other bonsai style, it is, however, the perfect type of tree from which to make a raft bonsai.

Step 2

With the tree remaining in its original container, gently but firmly wire the branches so that they are all pointing in the same direction, in this case to the right where the majority grow naturally. Begin wiring from the point where each branch joins the trunk, but do not wire around the trunk, as this is to become the root and it is well nigh impossible to remove the wire when once the trunk is rooted in the earth.

Step 3

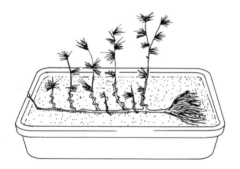

Carefully take the tree from its pot and turn it on its side so that the trunk is now in position to become the 'root' and the wired branches to become little trunks. Fill a shallow wooden box, seed tray or bonsai container with appropriate soil mixture and pot the new raft in what would be a horizontal position for the original tree. As a result, the old round rootball will be at one end of the new trunk root, and part of it will stick up above the surrounding soil.

Step 4

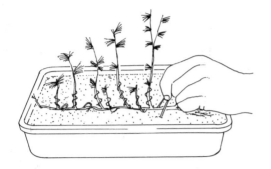

Make several incisions in the trunk root on the side that will rest in the soil and put a little rooting powder in each. Bend some short lengths of training wire in the shape of a hair pin and anchor the new root down in the soil with them, particularly in places where a curved trunk/root does not lie close to the surface. Pile up soil around the new trunk root and over the bottom half of the old rootball.

Step 5

When it is obvious that the raft has taken — as the little trunks put on growth and new roots can be seen under the top layer of soil — the old rootball will become superfluous and can simply be cut away. Do not be in too much of a hurry to repot the raft, however, as it can take between 1—5 years before it is sufficiently established to be put in its correct container.

Step 6

After this time, when the original branches are really beginning to look like individual trees and a mass of long roots have grown from the new root, the raft should be taken from its temporary home and potted down to a shallow bonsai tray. Holding the raft on its bed of soil, spread the roots out so that they radiate around the container and press soil particles in between them with a chopstick. Add more soil, building it up into a mound from the sides of the tray to the centre and thus displaying the raft to its best advantage.

The same raft bonsai as the one shown on page 84 here demonstrates the benefits of care and attention.

root quicker if treated as in Step 4. Do not make too many cuts or too deep and only apply a little hormone rooting powder. If the trunk curves away from the soil and does not remain firmly in place with thin stands of training wire, a few bent hairpins should do the trick. In a mature raft, like all "multi-trunk" bonsai styles, ideally no tree should align directly behind another when viewed directly from the front or from either side.

When the raft is firmly potted it can be put outside in the usual sheltered and partly-shaded position, then left for as long as it takes the new root to grow. Throughout this time, check the tree occasionally to see that it has not dried out or been knocked over and that it remains healthy. Water as required, but otherwise forget about the tree until such time as the new roots are showing through and you can happily dispense with what is remaining of the old rootball (Step 5).

It will then be an even longer period before you can pot the raft in its bonsai container (Step 6), certainly a year or more depending on the species. However, this does not mean that you should leave the raft entirely to its own devices for this length of time. As soon as the branches begin to thicken, taking on a more trunk-like form, they can be lightly pruned to whatever shape you have in mind. When these trunks are all growing up sturdily towards the light, you can take off the preliminary wiring on some and wire others into more natural forms so that the raft begins to adopt a more realistic shape instead of growing straight up like a row of soldiers.

The raft will remain in its first true bonsai container for several more years before it is ready to be potted down. Continue leaf and branch pruning and rewiring, as necessary, throughout this period. When a firm, flat root-ball is evident, this should be root-pruned and the raft potted into a shallow tray. Build up the soil from the sides to the plateau that is the root, so that the island-like qualities of the raft are all the more apparent.

Project 5
Group Plantings

Above: Photographed in the autumn, this is the same zelkova group as that on the left in spring.

Left: This fine group of three zelkova elms in full spring foliage look like a little copse through which the viewer is about to walk. This effect is achieved by placing the tallest tree at the back of the group and the smallest at the front.

Group plantings are a popular bonsai style, mainly because it is fairly easy to achieve an attractive forest-like profusion without too much effort and by use of comparatively inferior trees. The overall shape of a group is more important than the shape of individual trees, so that immature trees which are not sufficiently developed to stand alone as bonsai can be used to good effect. Indeed, if correctly positioned, several small young trees can look like one big, old specimen, and the effect is even more impressive when trees of different generations are combined so that, say, one mature bonsai is surrounded by young trees.

Many people also find group planting fairly

Step 1

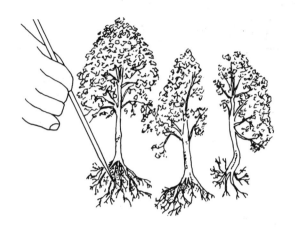

Prepare an uneven number of trees — in this case three zelkova elms — of sufficient size and similarity for a group planting. Ideally, all the trees should have been trained as bonsai in shallow pots for at least a year to grow relatively flat rootballs. Before potting, tease out the roots with a chopstick to unravel them and prune gently all round until a light fringe of roots remains, then spread these out evenly from the trunks.

Step 2

Choose a bonsai container large enough to accommodate however many trees are being used, of the correct shape to achieve the desired effect and prepare it in the usual way. Here, a woodland copse viewed close up is to be created in a relatively small, round pot of sufficient depth. Having pinpointed the position of each tree in relation to the rest, with the tallest at the rear, contour the soil accordingly. Press the soil down with a chopstick, a time-consuming process but one which gives a very firm base.

Step 3

As is always the case when trying to portray a close-up scene, pot the main tree towards the back of the container and continue heaping up the soil around its base. The remaining trees will be on slightly lower ground, in descending order, the whole impression being of a copse in a mountainous landscape, somewhat isolated from the rest of the forest.

Step 4

Here, the second sized tree has now been positioned slightly to the front and to the left of the tallest one. Now put the smallest tree in place, nearer the front rim of the container and a little to the right of the centre tree. The three zelkovas, as shown in the illustration opposite, are not symmetrical but form an unequal triangle with the steep right-hand side shorter than the sloping side. Ideally, when viewed from above, two of the trees on one side of the triangle should be close together, with the third some distance apart.

Step 5

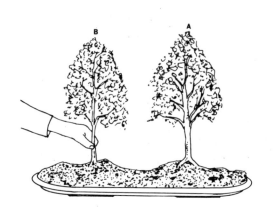

A larger group of eleven zelkovas is to be created, incorporating the previous three. Now the aim is to give the impression of a larger forest seen from a distance. The original group thus cannot remain in their present position as they must relate to the additional trees in size and placement to achieve the correct perspective. In a large, shallow tray, the soil is contoured to accommodate all eleven trees in relation to each other, with the largest tree, A, at the front of the centre line to the right. Put B to the left, further towards the rear.

Step 6

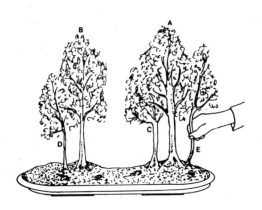

Now position the rest of the trees, in descending order of size, always relating them to their predecessors. Tree C, therefore, will be allied to A, that is a little to the left and the rear of the largest tree. Tree D will be placed in a similar position to the second largest tree B, and so on. Continue potting in this way until the smallest tree is finally closest to the back of the pot, representing the most distant tree to be seen in the forest.

simple and relaxing because most have their favourite wood from which to draw inspiration. Depending on the scene being recreated, most trees are suitable for groups. It is possible to mix species, but this is more difficult, especially when flowering and fruiting trees are used which do not mix well with others.

Specific plantings to give a copse or spinney effect, as in the first part of this project, need only a few trees, always an uneven number, if there are less than ten, and common evergreens such as pine, juniper and cryptomeria are popular. Maple, larch and zelkova elms are also much used in small groups. For a larger woodland scene, most deciduous species, like ash, beech, birch and hornbeam are excellent, although oak should be avoided. Remember that the bare shape of the trees in winter should equal the attraction of summer foliage. Beech, of course, hold their leaves in winter and have lovely grey trunks, as do ash.

Trees growing in forest-like profusion of twenty upwards are usually deciduous saplings with little or no intrinsic merit, but creating a memorable effect of depth and density when planted together. Even with such large numbers, accurate placement is important. Technically you should be able to see every tree from the front as well as from either side. Young trees, planted *en masse* by the handful in this way are sometimes referred to by the Japanese term of 'fist planting'. It is easier to achieve a good effect if the trunks are all fairly upright, but otherwise there are few inhibiting factors governing such grouping.

As discussed in relation to raft bonsai, group plantings should not be confused with other multi-trunk styles. When looking at group copses and spinneys, it is easy to mistake them for the Japanese style of clump planting in which single trees throw out several suckers which then are cultivated as individual trunks. However, the most commonly found trees for clump styles are maple, quince and yew which are not usually employed for groups.

Group plantings should reflect the growth habits of wild trees, surrounded by other forest trees, as they struggle towards the light. Obviously growth varies, due to the amount of light received, according to each tree's position in relation to its neighbours. Individual trees not overshadowed will have more abundant branches and foliage, and different parts of the same woodland will be at varying stages of growth depending on light intensity. For this reason, the overall shape of a group must never form an equilateral triangle, but should always have one relatively steep, short side and one long, sloping side (see Step 4).

This is a further reason why classically shaped individual bonsai, with well-spaced branches growing out evenly from the trunk on either side, are inappropriate for groups. Trees that are preferred for groups have long straight trunks, and the more trunks there are in a group the less branches will be needed. You should therefore look for trees with predominantly one-sided branching, particularly full outer branches and scanty inside ones.

Only seedlings and rooted cuttings can be successfully transplanted into groups without any prior training. All wild trees and most established nursery varieties benefit from being trained for a year or more in as shallow a tray as possible to flatten the rootball. This facilitates positioning and adjustment in relation to other trees when potting, as preconceived ideas change and you think it best to move a tree from its original site.

While waiting for the flat rootball to become established, train only those outer branches which will form the outline of the triangular shape. Never forget, however, that you might change your mind about their position, so do not remove any unwanted branches from the inside at this stage. Only when the tree is finally potted in place should you feel free to trim the branches. Basic rules to remember are that front-pointing branches only need retaining for trees near the front of the group, and back branches should be kept on trees at the rear of the container. Outside branches will, of course, remain at the outer extremities.

It is worth repeating here that in small groups the emphasis is less on the position of each tree than its relationship to the others in the group. Groups are viewed from the front at eye level, but certain attributes of good groups can be seen from the side and above. Never put one tree directly in front of another, and check from the side that the trunks do not cross over each other in an untidy manner. The side trees can lean outwards slightly as they do in the wild, and the whole group should lean slightly forwards.

Group plantings represent either close up or distant views. Generally small groups give the impression of small woods near to the viewer, while larger numbers portray whole forests far away, although these can be reversed. To create a close-up scene, as in the first part of this

The three zelkovas seen on pages 90 and 91 have now been incorporated in this large group on a shallow tray. The large middle tree from the threesome is third from the left in the left-hand group here, and the largest tree in the right-hand group was on the left of the threesome. The impression of a much larger woodland seen from a distance is created by putting the largest tree at the front and working back in descending order of size.

project, the smallest tree must be planted nearest the front of the container. The remaining trees, ascending in size, are placed in varying stages to the side and rear of the first one until the largest tree is positioned close to the back of the pot.

To recreate a more luxuriant, distant woodland, increase the number of trees and reverse the placings so that, in simple terms, the largest tree is nearest the front of the container and the smallest closest to the back. This effect is easier to achieve with many trees, and the bigger the differences in size, the greater the impression of depth. Tall, thin trees are best for this style, the tallest tree possessing the thickest trunk and the smallest tree the thinnest.

For this far-away style plant only the back two-thirds of a large shallow tray. Do not try to rush the basic preparation of the container (Step 2), as it can take hours to ensure that the soil is packed firm and contoured according to the position of the trees. Hold the trees upright when checking their placement, and remember that what might seem a difference of only a few centimetres may make a real change in the overall effect. Work against a plain background so that nothing detracts from the basic shape.

Above: Over thirty trident maple saplings grouped so that the smallest tree is at the front and the tallest is at the rear. This forms an illusion of a dark dense forest apparently very close at hand.

Left: This group of five larch appear to be on the middle ground of a relatively barren area. Again, the sense of distance is created by the largest tree being at the front of the group, to the left. Note how all the trees are planted to the rear of the tray.

With the tallest tree on the highest ground at the front of the group, it appears to be on a hill.

The value of a flat rootball will now be appreciated as it is all too easy for the trees to fall over in such shallow soil. Once potted, however, and sheltered from rough winds, the group should become stabilized in its container within six to eight weeks. During this time, while watching over it and watering as necessary, you will be able to gauge whether or not the planting is successful and what further training is needed. After the group has become established, you can decide whether it is sufficiently strong for it to stand alone, whether other trees should be added to form a larger group, or even whether it is not a success and would be best taken apart so that any of the trees with promise can be grown as individual bonsai.

The beauty of groups is this very flexibility. Equally, the same effect can be achieved with much less effort, by those people with less time, by creating a group planting in a window box. Phisically, this is much easier as you have a greater depth of soil to work with than in a shallow tray, and the visual effect will be very similar when viewed from inside a room.

Project 6
Bonsai Landscapes

Above: The components from which the desert scene opposite will be created. Grouped together on and around a cheap plastic tray are the lichen-covered rocks, and from left to right Opuntia brasiliensis, Crassula lycopodioides, Mammillaria prolifera, Stapelia variegata and Euphorbia mammillaris.

Left: The finished winter desert with white sand swirling up to the rocks around and out of which the cacti grow.

The Japanese love for encapsulating nature in miniature extends beyond growing individual dwarfed trees to the creation of equally impressive small-scale landscapes. This scaled-down reproduction of stylized natural scenes is not, however, a specialized sideline of bonsai production, but is covered by the two separate arts of bonkei and saikei.

Although both these skills can be generally summed up as the recollection of landscapes, or gardens in miniature, the main difference lies in the approach to the subject matter, as well as the diversity of materials and their uses. In simplistic terms, bonkei are idealized three-dimensional pictures of various aspects of country life throughout the year, created usually on a flat tray but also in less conventional containers, framed or free-standing. Bonkei can be 'live', when they incorporate living plants and frequently feature water as part of the design, or dry, when they are composed solely of artificial matter. Often artificial trees and plants are combined with real ones to achieve varying effects, as are such man-made features as tiny houses, temples and pagodas, bridges and boats and even miniature figures. Successful bonkei demands finesse in use of colour and in moulding keto, a peat-like substance from which mountains and other landscape contours are formed. It is very much a modeller's art, the practitioner being more closely allied to miniaturist painters

Step 1

Always bearing in mind the finished effect, the main static elements of the composition — in this case large rocks — are first put in position. Here they are placed to the back and sides of the shallow tray so that the living material can be grouped around them. To gain a natural effect, make sure that the striations on the rocks are running in the same direction. A layer of coarse drainage sand is scattered over the base of the tray which has been previously drilled to provide drainage holes.

Step 2

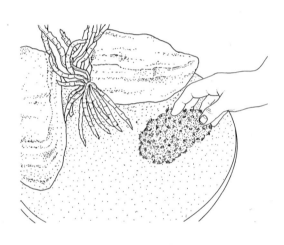

Try to create an impression of wide open spaces by careful placement of the living matter in relation to the rocks. Here, after a layer of cacti soil mix has been put all over the tray, the octopus-like euphorbia is placed in the middle of the rocks, as if growing through them. Find the best position for a clump of dumpy mammillaria, in the foreground as if close to the viewer.

Step 3

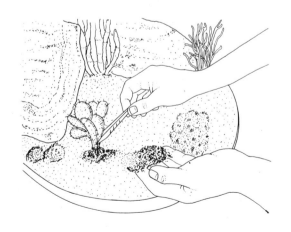

Do not attempt to plant a prickly cactus like this opuntia by hand, as you will be covered in dozens of tiny, painful spines that are difficult to dislodge and may work into the skin. Pick up a cactus at its base with a pair of tweezers and hold it firmly in place as you heap more soil around the roots. This is particularly important with plants, like cacti, which have very short root systems, so must be securely positioned.

Step 4

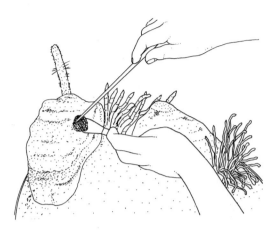

For an even more natural effect, as if the plants are actually growing on the rocks, find a suitable cavity and fill it with soil. If the crevice is shallow, hold a small amount of soil on a spatula close to the hole and firm it in place with a chopstick. A large cactus, in danger of falling over, can be fixed in place with lengths of wire and a metal sinker (Project 3, Steps 3 and 4). The tall, spiky stapelia has been put behind the rocks, as if growing over them.

Step 5

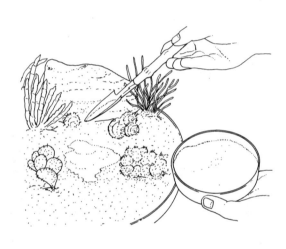

With all the plants in place, complete the scene by sprinkling on coloured sand to represent the overall surface. On top of a layer of yellow sand used as desert background, white sand is added to give an impression of light snowfall. It is put on with a trowel which avoids too much sand falling on top of the cacti. The sand can be built up in large mounds to denote snow drifts, as here, or used to create sand dunes, hills, etc.

Step 6

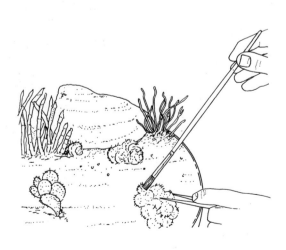

Any excess sand which does spill onto the cacti should be removed, although this may prove difficult as it sticks to the spines and attempts to dust it away can dislodge the precariously rooted plants. The best method is to hold the cactus in place with tweezers, and use a fine hair brush to wipe away any stray sand particles and generally tidy the scene.

The components for constructing the meadow landscape below. Back, left to right: rooted conifer cuttings, potting compost, box tree; front, left to right: coarse sand, jasmine, moss.

and sculptors than to gardeners, although the inspiration is drawn from the highest appreciation of nature.

Saikei, a much younger pursuit, uses only living materials such as seedlings and rooted cuttings, in conjunction with small rocks and stones, to form tiny landscapes. Less formal, with fewer rules than the older arts, it usually appeals to those of a more adventurous and romantic nature.

Both saikei and bonkei are, as noted earlier in relation to group plantings, very different from Western miniature gardens which are generally housed in deep tubs such as half barrels or old sinks. The other major difference is that the plants used are dwarfed strains, bred specially for the purpose, which do not grow beyond a certain size and therefore require little specialized cultivation after the initial scheme has been established. Some European and American miniatures do incorporate occasional features such as tiny stone ornaments, an arch or trellis for climbers or even, if the occasion demands, a small windmill or other building. The main emphasis, however, is usually on the planting and the relationship of the trees, flowers and foliage. To the Western mind, a garden is a garden and that is what is produced in miniature as in actuality.

Just as the more rigid Japanese bonsai styles do not appeal to Western sensibilities, likewise some of the intricately fashioned bonkei and the simple form of saikei are similarly not appreciated. In this section we have, therefore, simply attempted to summarize the main ideas behind Japanese miniatures together with some basic methods of planting and display. Anyone interested in growing bonsai can then, if wished, incorporate the tiny trees into landscapes of their own making, along with other plants and materials.

The path winds into the soft hills and the hedge recedes into the distance in this evocative country scene where the contours of the soil are as important to the overall effect as the individual trees.

The main difference between this tri-part project and the previous one is that in group plantings, whichever trees are used, the end result is virtually always the same kind of scene, despite the varying number of trees, but here the landscapes are never the same. However many bonsai are *grouped* on a shallow tray, and whether they conjure up a copse, spinney or dense woodland, in the end they represent part of a forest. In a tray landscape, however, while a single tree, two or three windswept ones, or even a small coppice might be included, they are but single elements in the total environment. As a lone bonsai aims to recapture one memorable aspect of nature, the miniature 'gardens' attempt to recreate a whole scene. Thus the trees, however attractive in their one right, do not stand alone but complement other equally important features such as water, rock formation or the contours of the earth.

The three landscapes depicted here — a desert under snow, a fertile plain at the foot of rolling hills and a rugged coastal bay — should only be considered as representing an unlimited number of such memorable scenes. They are also personal reconstructions; each would be different in the eye of the beholder. The desert is a recreation of a winter's day in Mexico, where the contrast of the white snow over the yellow sand left an indelible mark on the inner eye of a person accustomed to more temperate climes. The meadow, with its hedge, trees and path leading to the gentle slopes, was based on part of the Sussex downland, but could equally apply to parts of Vermont or the Loire Valley, and the supposed Scottish headland stands for all such wild coast.

It is best, however, to recall a landscape with particular personal associations than to try to produce a 'typical' scene. If your memory fails, there is no harm in consulting a photograph of the place, but do not be side-tracked into including every feature instead of simply bringing back a general mood. As with bonsai, you are not merely creating an exact small replica but an idealized scene in which all the elements harmonize with one another.

The most successful tray landscapes are those with a heightened sense of perspective. A sense of distance is not so vital in a close-up view, but most memorable scenes include a foreground and a distant vista with a focal point somewhere between the two. The size and positioning of the trees and rocks is a major factor here. As with group plantings, larger trees or objects in the

Step 1

Contrary to expectation, a real sense of perspective can be gained in a narrow container. In a tray just 30 × 45 cm (12 × 18in) as here, skilled planting can evoke distances of up to 16 km (10 miles). Place the largest feature in the scene, here the dwarf box tree, near the front of the tray and to one side. Heap up the soil around the base to secure it. Anything smaller, positioned to the rear of this 20 cm (8 in) tree, will look as if it is receding into the near distance.

Step 2

Landscaping the earth to form distant rolling hills is a fundamental factor in the success of this meadow scene. At the back of the tray, add enough soil to the overall layer to raise it above the rim. Use your hands to mould gentle contours in this raised earth and pat the slopes into a smooth surface with the fingers.

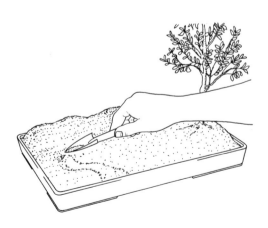

Step 3

Interest is added, and the idea of perspective enhanced, by the addition of a little path which meanders up to the hills. Take a little trowel full of light-coloured sand and sprinkle it in a curving motion from the front edge of the tray to where the 'hills' begin. At the start the path should be about 5 cm (2in) wide, gradually becoming narrower and lighter over a distance of some 10 cm (4in) until it is merely a grain or so thick where it disappears.

Step 4

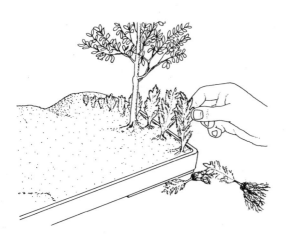

Make a hedge to accompany the large tree from several young rooted cuttings of any appropriate species. You will need relatively large numbers for a thick hedge, in a range of sizes. To reinforce the impression that the hedge too is receding, grade the cuttings or seedlings and plant the largest near the front of the tray, going down in size to the smallest at the rear.

Step 5

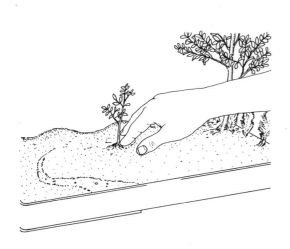

As more elements are added, it will become apparent that others are needed. At this stage the large tree has been balanced by the hedge on one side, but is separated from the path to the extent that the two do not relate. By putting in a smaller tree such as this jasmine, placed behind and to the left of the box tree, a more harmonious composition is achieved, and the sense of perspective heightened.

Step 6

Complete the scene by bringing in different colours and textures. Distribute clumps of moss round the trees to help secure them and to prevent water loss. Lighter green, springy moss for the general surface makes good substitute grass, while darker shades of moss over the contoured slopes add to the 'reality' of the distant hills.

foreground and smaller ones towards the back, give an impression of depth. The same principle applies to features such as paths and streams which start wide and gradually taper off as they supposedly go farther away.

The first essential for this type of garden is the container. Avoid the pretty, more expensive type of tray, perhaps lacquered, as very little can be seen once they are covered with soil. Also, the trays must have adequate drainage holes which should be drilled or punched in, so a colourful, relatively inexpensive plastic or tin tray is perfectly adequate.

The type of soil used, as always should reflect the material growing in it. Obviously a specific cacti mix is used for the desert scene, but a general mixture of sterilized soil and soilless compost is normally acceptable. Clay and peat make a firm base for plants on rocks or in cavities. The art of forming contours with the soil is vital to good tray landscapes, a point where bonkei skills are useful, although here it is the action of the hands and fingers, patting down and

smoothing in place, which is more important than shaping with a tool.

Rocks and stones of varying shapes and sizes are perhaps the next most important component. Look for them at the same time as when searching for suitable homes for rock-clinging bonsai, although the landscape rocks are generally smaller. And, whereas a single rock on which to put a bonsai can have strikingly individual qualities, unless you are seeking a particularly singular peak or cliff face, it is better if the rocks in each garden are similar in colour and texture. To back up the impression of real cliffs, make sure that when the rocks are positioned on the tray, the striations — lines running through them — are all going in the same direction.

Various kinds of sand are an essential part of tray landscapes. Again, do not use sand from the beach, but buy horticultural sand. A coarse variety is frequently mixed with the soil to aid drainage, and others of different colours and consistencies can be used to portray all kinds of surfaces. Much depends on personal taste. While a bright blue type of fish tank gravel may seem ideal for a small stream or pond to one person, it may not appeal to another. Experiment with what is to hand, so long as it cannot harm the living matter. Plain grit from the roads, for example, makes a good basic scree and a few grains of washing powder add a realistic touch of 'white horses' to the tops of curling waves.

Moss is also very useful when creating minilandscapes. As well as denoting colour variations and different surfaces, it also helps bind the shallow soil together and keeps it moist. You can simply take up moss and press it in position to create an immediate effect, but it may die back before becoming established if the conditions are not right. If you can contain your impatience at wishing to finish off the scene, put small lumps of moss in place on the surface soil, cover with another light layer of soil, firm down and water. The new moss should begin to sprout in about ten days.

If moss is in short supply, make sure of an available source by growing your own. Leave

a lump to dry, then pound it finely in a mortar or pass through a sieve. Add about one third moss to two-thirds soil and put on top of a layer of soil, pressing in place and spraying regularly with water so that it never dries out. The moss will begin to form in a little over two weeks.

Live material used in tray landscapes depends on the scene in question. Cacti, naturally, are used in a desert scene, and a compact variety of heather would be at home on an upland. Once again, do not be too literal in your choice of plants for different situations. The larger tree in our English meadow landscape was a box and the smaller a jasmine, hardly a typical combination but one that *looked* right in context. If you intend to alter the landscape from time to time, or even to renew it entirely, you will naturally be

The bleak coastal bay (below) with waves washing onto a deserted beach where only the rocks stand firm against the powerful winds and the stunted trees bow in submission is formed from such simple objects as rocks, sand, moss and seedlings (facing page), all welded together by artistic skills and the power of the imagination.

Step 1

From a collection of small to medium sized rocks and pebbles, choose three or four of different shapes, but of similar colour and texture, which fit together well. Cover the surface of a plastic or tin tray with a layer of clay and peat mixture. Position the rocks in a natural-looking formation, curving round about two-thirds of the rear of the tray, making sure that the lines on them are all running the same way.

Step 2

Press home any remaining soil mix into the crevices between the rocks. Using varying shades of moss, press clumps in place behind, on top of and at the base of the rocks as appropriate. Powdered moss, if sown correctly, will give an all-over cover within weeks, but the landscape will look rather bare until it starts to grow.

Step 3

Add a living element to the scene by including one or more tiny trees. If you do not want to disturb a bonsai, use rooted cuttings again. The needle juniper shoots being planted here look very like the type of trees to be found in such a wild situation. Plant them at a slight angle, at the side or top of the rocks to make it look as if they are bending in the wind.

Step 4

Form the beach in the foreground by trickling light-coloured sand of varying depths in a semi-circle beneath the rocks. The colour and thickness of the sand can be altered as befits the scene, with perhaps a darker shade round the 'water's edge' and a line of white sand at the foot of the rocks where it might be driest. To complete the picture, a swirling layer of heavier greyish sand round the perimeter represents the sea, with a few grains of washing powder for waves.

reluctant to risk valuable or immature bonsai. When only small trees are needed, it is best to use seedlings or rooted cuttings of various sizes. These may achieve a surprisingly realistic effect, as well as providing a point of interest as they mature. Equally, it is not such a loss if they fail to take.

If a larger tree is required, take the opportunity to include some of your less successful bonsai which do not quite make the grade as individual trees, are too advanced to include in a multi-group planting, and may well take on new meaning in a landscaped setting. As the tree has

to grow in relatively shallow soil on the tray, it is essential that it has already received training in a bonsai container and has a comparatively flat rootball.

You can thus adapt your bonsai skills to a related form of creativity. The beauty of this type of miniature is that a scene can be put together — and even undone if required — within hours. All kinds of containers and settings are permissible, from a window box to the shallow top of a wall. And an indoor arrangement makes an unusual change to greet guests instead of the conventional flowers.

Further Information

BOOKS

There are far too many gardening books with general advice on tree cultivation to be included here. Similarly, of the available books on bonsai and its allied arts, many are rather esoteric for the general taste, being direct translations from the Japanese. The following titles are to be recommended for their sound basic approach towards all trees and bonsai growing in particular.

ADAMS, Peter SUCCESSFUL BONSAI GROWING (Ward Lock, London 1978)

HART, C. BRITISH TREES IN COLOUR (Michael Joseph, London 1973)

HILLIER, H. (Ed) HILLIER'S MANUAL OF TREES AND SHRUBS (David & Charles, Newton Abbot 1978)

HIROTA, J. BONKEI: TRAY LANDSCAPES (Phaidon, Oxford; Harper & Row, New York; Kodansha International Ltd, Tokyo 1974)

KAWAMOTO, T. SAIKEI: LIVING LANDSCAPES IN MINIATURE (Phaidon, Oxford; Harper & Row, New York; Kodansha, Tokyo)

KAWASUMI, M. BONSAI WITH AMERICAN TREES (Phaidon, Oxford; Harper & Row, New York; Kodansha, Tokyo 1978)

LARKIN, H. J. BONSAI FOR BEGINNERS (Angus & Robertson, London 1976)

MURATA, K. and K. BONSAI (Hoikusha Publishing, Osaka 1977)

WALKER, Linda M. BONSAI (Gifford, London 1978)

SUPPLIERS

General nurseries have been recommended throughout this book as providing many suitable trees to grow as bonsai. Also, many major seedsmen sell bonsai tree seeds, either direct or through general retail outlets, garden centres, etc. There are, however, a number of specialist bonsai nurseries, several of which import trees direct from Japan and which also supply tools and literature.

Bromage & Young Ltd, Wildacre, Brookhurst Road, Cranleigh, Surrey

Glenside Bonsai, 98 Richmond Road, Freemantle, Southampton, Hants

Price & Adams, Cherry Trees, 22 Burnt Hill Road, Wrecclesham, Farnham, Surrey

Sei-yo Kan Bonsai (J.A.S.B. Ltd), 20 Battersea High Street, London SW11

Thompson & Morgan Ltd, London Road, Ipswich, Suffolk

Tokonoma Bonsai, 14 London Road, Shenley, Radlett, Herts

BONSAI SOCIETIES

Too many localized bonsai groups exist to list here. However, the main national societies can recommend area, state, or even town associations and local suppliers.

Bonsai Societies in the UK:

Bonsai Kai of the Japan Society of London Hon. Sec. Japan Society of London, 656 Grand Buildings, Trafalgar Square, London WC2

Hon. Sec. Bonsai Kai of the Japan Society of London, 39 West Square, London SE11

British Bonsai Association, 23 Nimrod Road, London SW16

Bonsai Societies in the USA:

American Bonsai Society, 953 South Shore Drive, Lake Waukomis, Parkville, Mo. 64151

Bonsai Clubs International, 480 Oxford Street, Arcadia, California 91006

Bonsai Society of Greater New York Inc., Box E, The Bronx, New York, N. York 10466

California Bonsai Society, PO Box 78211, Los Angeles, California 90016